Searchlight BOOKS™

How Does
Your Body
Work?

Your

Nervous System

Joelle Riley

Lerner Publications Company
Minneapolis

Lerner Publications Company
A division of Lerner Publishing Group, Inc.
241 First Avenue North
Minneapolis, MN 55401 U.S.A.

Website address: www.lernerbooks.com

Library of Congress Cataloging-in-Publication Data

Riley, Joelle.
    Your nervous system / by Joelle Riley.
       p.   cm. — (Searchlight books™—How does your body work?)
    Includes index.
    ISBN 978–0–7613–7450–3 (lib. bdg. : alk. paper)
    1. Nervous system—Juvenile literature. I. Title.
QP361.5.R54 2013
612.8—dc23   2011044176

Manufactured in the United States of America
1 – CG – 7/15/12

Contents

Chapter 1

THE CENTRAL SYSTEM

Your body has many systems.
A system is a way of doing things.
Your body's systems help it do the
things it needs to do to stay alive.

Your body is like a
complicated machine.
What are some of
the things happening
inside your body?

Your muscles and bones help you move. Your heart pumps blood through your body. Your lungs bring in air. And your stomach breaks down the food you eat. But what keeps all these systems working?

Your body's systems help you do things such as playing games.

Command Center

Your nervous system controls all the other systems. It keeps track of everything that happens in your body. Your nervous system tells your other systems what to do. Without your nervous system, none of your other systems could do their jobs.

Your nervous system keeps all your other systems working. It also helps you to think.

But your nervous system does much more than just control your other systems. Your nervous system helps you dance. It helps you solve puzzles. It helps you laugh. It helps you remember the names of your friends. It helps you see flowers and hear music. It even helps you dream.

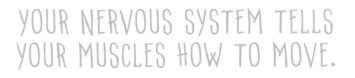

YOUR NERVOUS SYSTEM TELLS YOUR MUSCLES HOW TO MOVE.

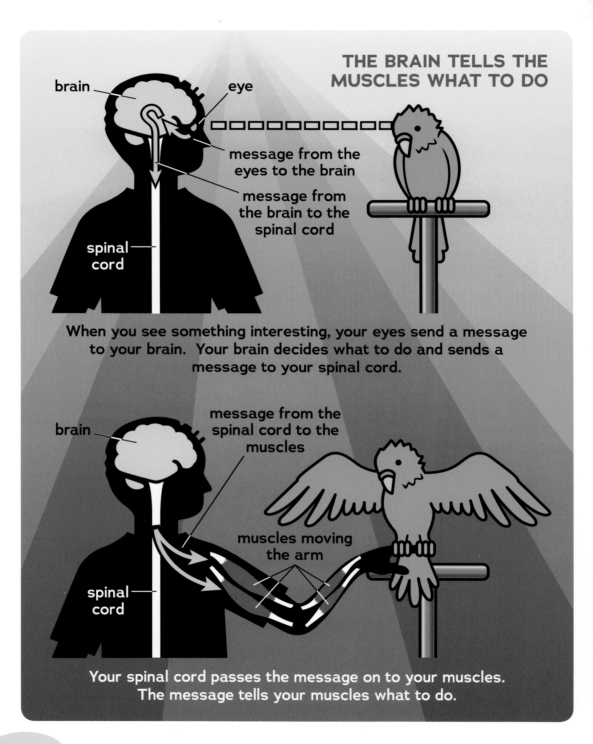

THE BRAIN TELLS THE MUSCLES WHAT TO DO

brain

eye

message from the eyes to the brain

message from the brain to the spinal cord

spinal cord

When you see something interesting, your eyes send a message to your brain. Your brain decides what to do and sends a message to your spinal cord.

message from the spinal cord to the muscles

brain

muscles moving the arm

spinal cord

Your spinal cord passes the message on to your muscles. The message tells your muscles what to do.

Parts of the Nervous System

Your nervous system is made up of your nerves, your spinal cord, and your brain. Nerves carry messages to and from all parts of your body. Your spinal cord connects your nerves to your brain. Your brain thinks. It keeps track of everything that happens in your body. It tells the other body systems what to do.

This picture shows the inside of a person's head and neck. The colored parts of the picture show the brain and the spinal cord.

Chapter 2

NERVES

Your nerves are made up of special cells called nerve cells. A nerve cell's job is to collect messages and pass them on.

A microscope was used to take this picture of nerve cells. What parts does a nerve cell have?

Each nerve cell has a body, a tail, and branching parts that look like hairs. A nerve cell's hairs collect a message. The message travels through the hairs. It goes through the cell's body. Then it moves down the tail. The tail passes the message to the hairs on another nerve cell.

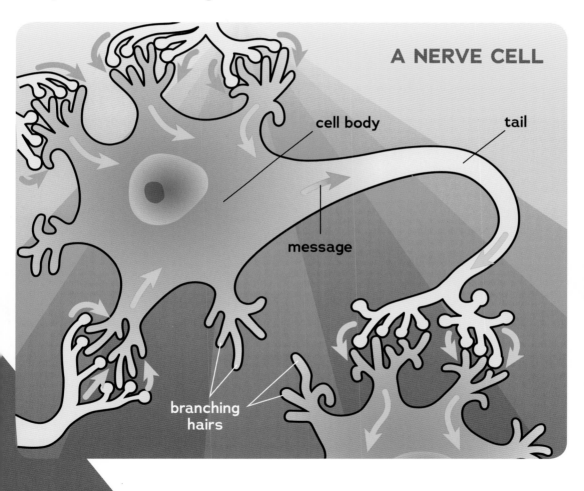

A NERVE CELL

cell body

tail

message

branching hairs

The Size of Nerve Cells

Nerve cells are tiny. You would need a microscope to see one. But many nerve cells are bundled together to make nerves. Nerves are big enough to be seen without a microscope.

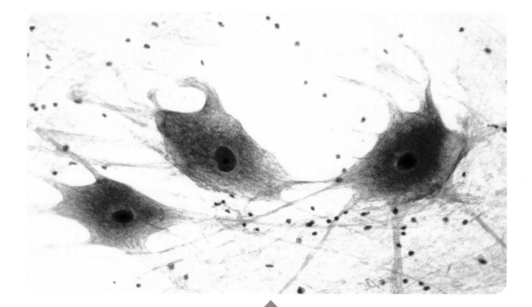

THIS PICTURE SHOWS THREE
NERVE CELLS UP CLOSE.

Receptors

Some nerve cells collect messages from your skin or from other parts of your body. These nerve cells are called receptors. Receptors collect information from the world and from your body.

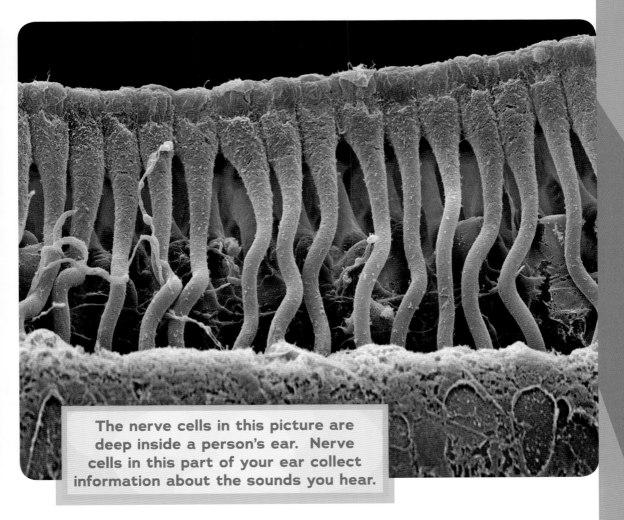

The nerve cells in this picture are deep inside a person's ear. Nerve cells in this part of your ear collect information about the sounds you hear.

Receptors in your skin, ears, eyes, nose, and tongue collect messages from the world around you. Other receptors collect messages from inside your body. Nerve cells pass these messages to your spinal cord or your brain.

Special cells inside the eye collect information about things that you see.

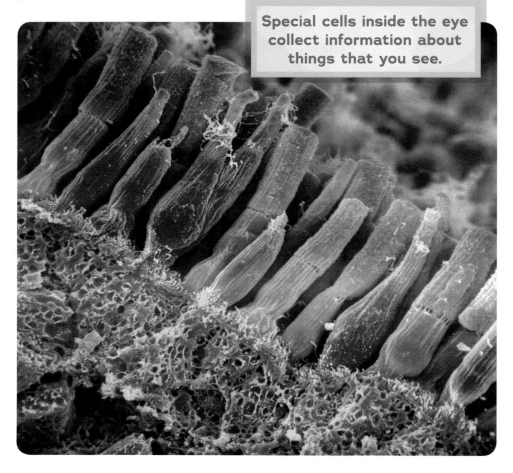

Other nerve cells collect messages from your brain. Then the nerve cells carry the messages to your muscles or to other parts of your body.

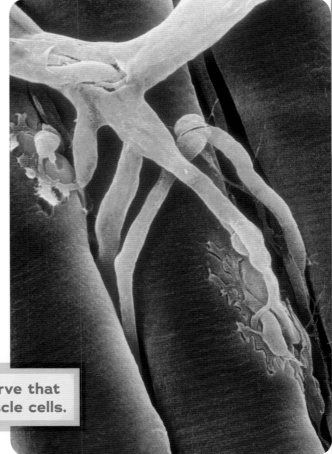

This picture shows a nerve that carries messages to muscle cells.

Message Center

A nerve is like a telephone cable that is made up of many different wires. A telephone cable can send many calls at once, because each wire can send one call. A nerve can send many messages at once too. Each nerve cell can send a different message.

Nerves are in every part of your body. Messages travel very quickly through your nerves. A message can travel from your brain to your foot faster than you can blink your eyes!

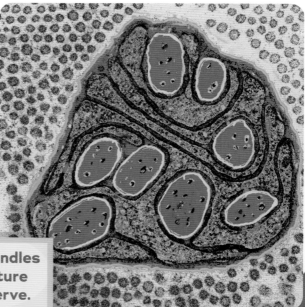

Each nerve is made of bundles of nerve cells. This picture shows the inside of a nerve.

Chapter 3

THE SPINAL CORD

Your spinal cord is a thick bundle of nerves. It looks like a white rope. The spinal cord got its name from the spine. Another name for the spine is the backbone. Your spinal cord fits through holes in your backbone. The hard backbone keeps your spinal cord from being hurt.

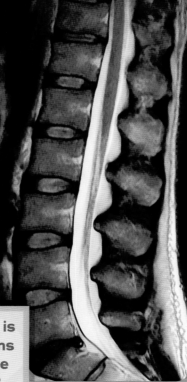

The solid blue line in this picture is the spinal cord. The blue sections are the backbone. How does the backbone help the spinal cord?

Bundles of nerves from all over your body meet up with the spinal cord. Some of the nerves collect messages from your spinal cord. They pass these messages to other parts of your body. Other nerves pass messages to the spinal cord. Your spinal cord sends these messages on to your brain.

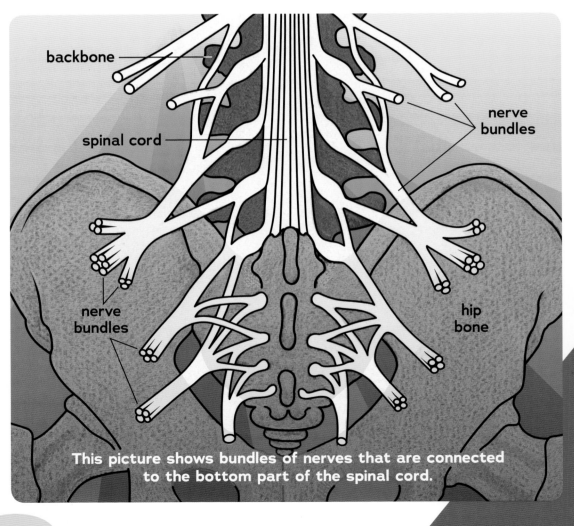

backbone

nerve bundles

spinal cord

nerve bundles

hip bone

This picture shows bundles of nerves that are connected to the bottom part of the spinal cord.

Chapter 4

THE BRAIN

Your brain is the part of your body that makes you who you are. Your brain helps you speak. And it helps you understand what others are saying. It remembers the things you have done, seen, and learned. Your brain makes you feel happy or sad. It decides what your favorite colors and foods are. It helps you learn to ride a bike. And it keeps the rest of your body working well.

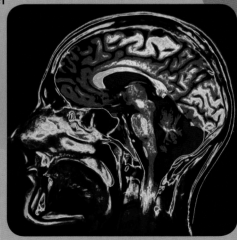

The brain has many different parts. What are some of the things the brain does?

Skull

Your brain is very soft. But your skull protects your brain. Your skull is made of hard bones. The bones fit together tightly. They keep your brain from being hurt, even if you fall and bump your head.

Inside your skull, your brain floats in clear liquid. The liquid keeps your brain from banging against your skull and being hurt.

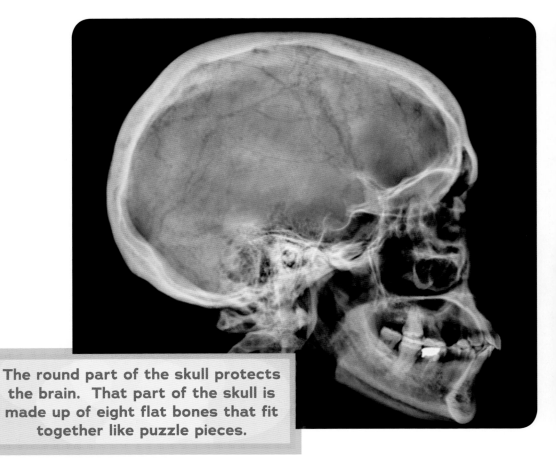

The round part of the skull protects the brain. That part of the skull is made up of eight flat bones that fit together like puzzle pieces.

Your brain has three main parts. The three parts are called the brain stem, the cerebellum, and the cerebrum. Each part has important jobs to do.

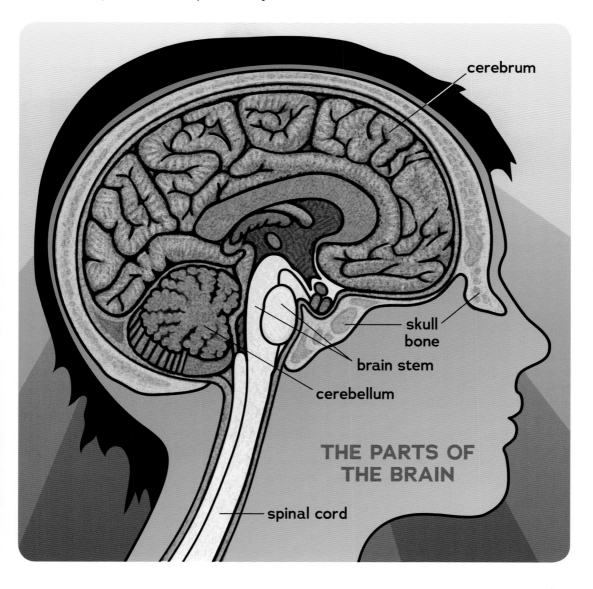

cerebrum

skull
bone

brain stem

cerebellum

THE PARTS OF THE BRAIN

spinal cord

Brain Stem

Your brain stem passes messages between your brain and your spinal cord. Your brain stem controls the movement of your head and neck too.

The things that your body does on its own are controlled by your brain stem. It keeps your heart beating and your lungs breathing. It controls how the food you eat is broken down. It controls sleeping and dreaming. It controls swallowing, vomiting, sneezing, coughing, and hiccuping too!

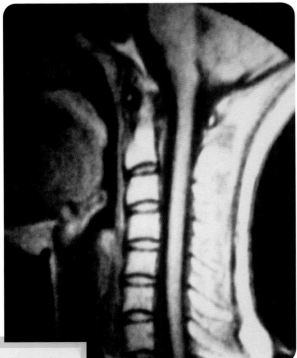

The brain stem is attached to the spinal cord at the top of the neck.

Cerebellum

Your cerebellum controls how you move. It helps you keep your balance. It also stores memories of how to do things, such as eating with a fork or riding a skateboard.

YOUR CEREBELLUM HELPS YOU KEEP YOUR BALANCE WHEN YOU RIDE A SKATEBOARD.

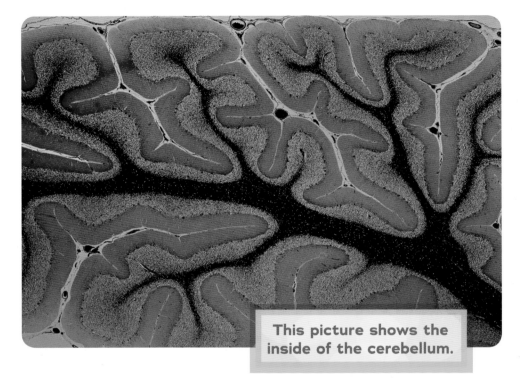

This picture shows the inside of the cerebellum.

Cortex

Your cerebrum is the biggest part of your brain. The outside layer of the cerebrum is called the cortex. The cortex has deep wrinkles. The wrinkles help the cortex to take up less space. It's like crumpling a big sheet of paper into a tiny ball to make the paper smaller.

An adult's brain weighs about 3 pounds (1.3 kilograms). It is about the size of a big grapefruit.

Your cortex is the part of your brain that does most of your thinking. It receives messages from your eyes, ears, nose, tongue, and skin. It saves memories and makes decisions. It also helps to control your muscles.

Cerebrum

Your cerebrum is divided into two halves that look like the halves of a walnut. The left half of your cerebrum controls the muscles of the right side of your body. And the right half of your cerebrum controls the muscles of the left side of your body.

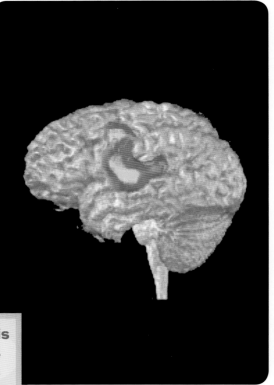

The bright areas in this picture are the parts of the cerebrum that help a person talk.

Each half of your cerebrum is good at doing different things. The left half is best at talking, reading, and doing math problems. The right half is best at making music and art, understanding shapes, imagining, and making jokes.

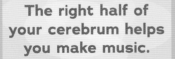

The right half of your cerebrum helps you make music.

Chapter 5

WORKING TOGETHER

Your nerves, spinal cord, and brain work together. By working together, they keep your body running well.

The parts of your nervous system work together. How do messages travel through your nervous system?

Your body collects millions of messages every day. Your nervous system ignores most of them. But every so often, a receptor collects an important message. Then the receptor passes the message on to a nerve. The nerve passes the message to your spinal cord. And your spinal cord passes it on to your brain. Your brain decides what to do about it.

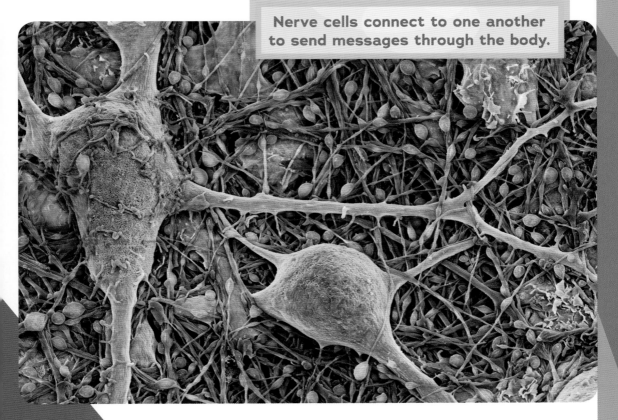

Nerve cells connect to one another to send messages through the body.

Smells

Suppose receptors in your nose pick up a message. It's an interesting message. Your nerves carry the message to your brain. Your cerebrum goes through all of its smell memories. Aha! The message means that cookies are baking! Your cerebrum remembers that cookies are good to eat. It decides that you should go and get one.

When your nose smells freshly baked cookies, your nervous system sends a message to your brain.

Your cerebellum takes over. It figures out how you need to move to go to the kitchen. Moments after your nose smelled the cookies, you are eating one.

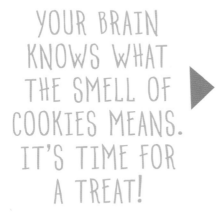

YOUR BRAIN KNOWS WHAT THE SMELL OF COOKIES MEANS. IT'S TIME FOR A TREAT!

Spinal Cord to the Rescue

All of this happens quickly. But sometimes there's an emergency. Your body needs to act even more quickly to keep you from being hurt. Then your spinal cord comes to the rescue.

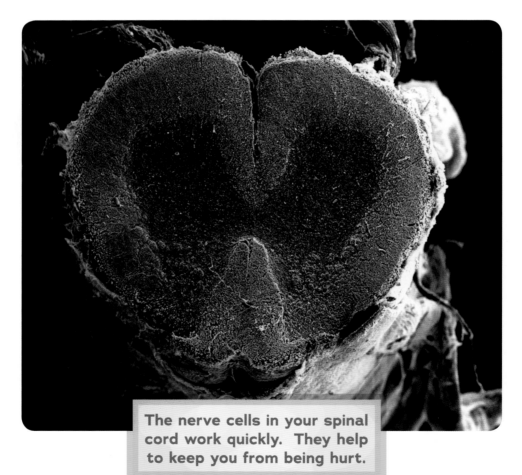

The nerve cells in your spinal cord work quickly. They help to keep you from being hurt.

Your spinal cord helps to protect you by causing reflexes. A reflex is something your body does even though you didn't think about doing it.

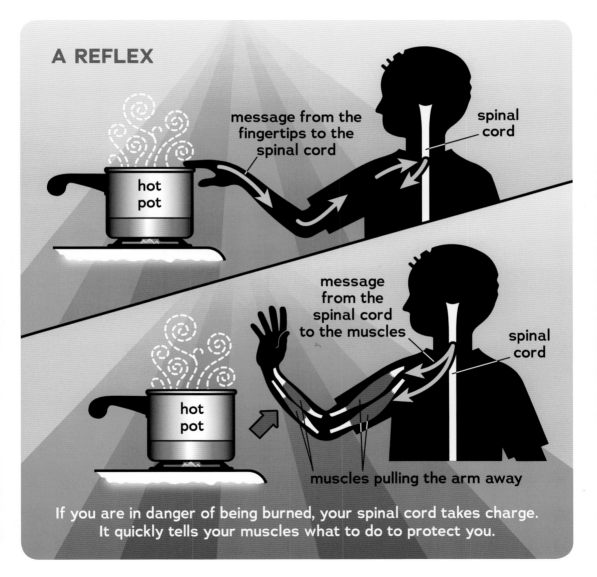

A REFLEX

message from the fingertips to the spinal cord

spinal cord

hot pot

message from the spinal cord to the muscles

spinal cord

hot pot

muscles pulling the arm away

If you are in danger of being burned, your spinal cord takes charge. It quickly tells your muscles what to do to protect you.

If you touch a hot pot, nerves in your skin send an emergency message. The message travels to your spinal cord. There is no time to send a message to your brain and ask it what to do. So your spinal cord causes a reflex. It sends a message to your arm muscles.

Touching something that is very hot can cause a bad burn.

The Message

The message tells your muscles to pull your hand away from the pot. The muscles tighten, and your hand jerks away from the pot. The message travels so quickly that your hand pulls away before you even feel the heat! The spinal cord's fast action helps to keep you from being badly burned.

If you touch a hot pot, your spinal cord makes you pull your hand away fast!

In Control

Your nervous system controls everything you do. It keeps your body running smoothly. It helps you remember where you live. It helps you make up stories and eat ice cream. It helps you throw a ball. It helps you decide what is right and what is wrong.

Your nervous system makes you different from everyone else in the world. It makes you special.

Your nervous system helps you taste ice cream.

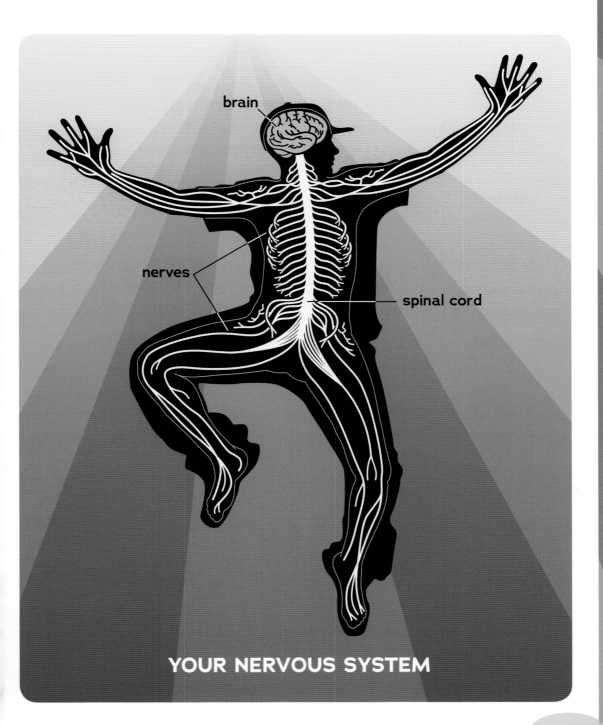

brain

nerves

spinal cord

YOUR NERVOUS SYSTEM

Glossary

brain: the organ that keeps track of everything in the body

brain stem: the part of the brain that controls things the body does on its own

cerebellum: the part of the brain that controls how the body moves

cerebrum: the biggest part of the brain. It is divided into two halves. Each half is good at different things.

cortex: the wrinkly layer on the outside of the brain. It is the part of the brain that thinks, saves memories, and makes decisions.

nerve: a bundle of cells that carries messages around the body

receptor: a nerve cell that collects information from the world and the body

reflex: something the body does automatically, without thinking about it

skull: the hard bones in the head that protect the brain

spinal cord: a bundle of nerve cells that runs through the backbone. It connects nerves to the brain.

Learn More about the Nervous System

Books

Capaccio, George. *Nervous System*. Tarrytown, NY: Marshall Cavendish Benchmark, 2010. The author discusses the parts of the body that make up the nervous system, what can go wrong with the nervous system, and how problems can be treated.

Johnson, Rebecca L . *Your Muscular System*. Minneapolis: Lerner Publications Company, 2013. Learn about how the muscular system works with the nervous system.

Parker, Steve. *Nervous System*. Mankato, MN: New Forest Press, 2011. Parker introduces the nervous system, explains its parts and how they function, and describes how it works with the five senses.

Taylor-Butler, Christine. *The Nervous System*. New York: Children's Press, 2008. This title discusses the nervous system, including its purpose, parts, and functions.

Websites

IMCPL Kids' Info Guide: Nervous System
http://www.imcpl.org/kids/guides/health/nervoussystem.html
This page from the Indianapolis Marion County Public Library has a list of resources you can use to learn more about the nervous system.

KidsHealth: How the Body Works
http://kidshealth.org/kid/htbw/htbw_main_page.html
Click on the brain box to watch a movie, read articles, and solve a word puzzle about this important body part.

Neuroscience for Kids
http://faculty.washington.edu/chudler/neurok.html
This lively site includes facts about the brain and nervous system along with experiments, activities, and links to other websites.

Index

Photo Acknowledgments

The images in this book are used with the permission of: © Jim Carter/Photo Researchers/Getty Images, p. 4; © Photo Researchers/Getty Images, p. 5; © Jupiterimages/FoodPix/Getty Images, p. 6; © Francisco Cruz/SuperStock, p. 7; © Laura Westlund/Independent Picture Service, pp. 8, 11, 18, 21, 33; 37; © Derek Berwin/Stone/Getty Images, p. 9; © Dr. Dennis Kunkel/Dennis Kunkel Microscopy, Inc./Visuals Unlimited, Inc., p. 10; © Ed Reschke/Peter Arnold/Getty Images, p. 12; © SPL/Photo Researchers, Inc., pp. 13, 32; © Omikron/Photo Researchers, Inc., p. 14; © Don W. Fawcett/Photo Researchers/Getty Images, p. 15; © Sercomi/Photo Researchers, Inc., p. 16; © Gustoimages/ Photo Researchers, Inc., p. 17; © Geoff Tompkinson/Science Photo Library/Getty Images, p. 19; © Zephyr/Science Photo Library/Getty Images, p. 20; © Hammersmith Hospital Medical School/ Photo Researchers, Inc., p. 22; © MoMo Productions/Taxi/Getty Images, p. 23; © Manfred P. Kage/ Photo Researchers, Inc., p. 24; © Dr. P. Marazzi/Photo Researchers, Inc., p. 25; © Scientifica ADEAR/ Visuals Unlimited, Inc., p. 26; © Xavier Gallego Morell/Dreamstime.com, p. 27; © PhotoDisc Royalty Free by Getty Images, p. 28; © Thomas Deerinck/Photo Researchers, Inc., p. 29; © Todd Strand/ Independent Picture Service, p. 30; © Monkey Business Images/Dreamstime.com, p. 31; © Nana Twumasi/Independent Picture Service, p. 34; © Purestock/Getty Images, p. 35; © VisitBritain/Rod Edwards/Britain On View/Getty Images, p. 36.

Front cover: © MedicalRF.com/Getty Images.

Main body text set in Adrianna Regular 14/20.
Typeface provided by Chank.